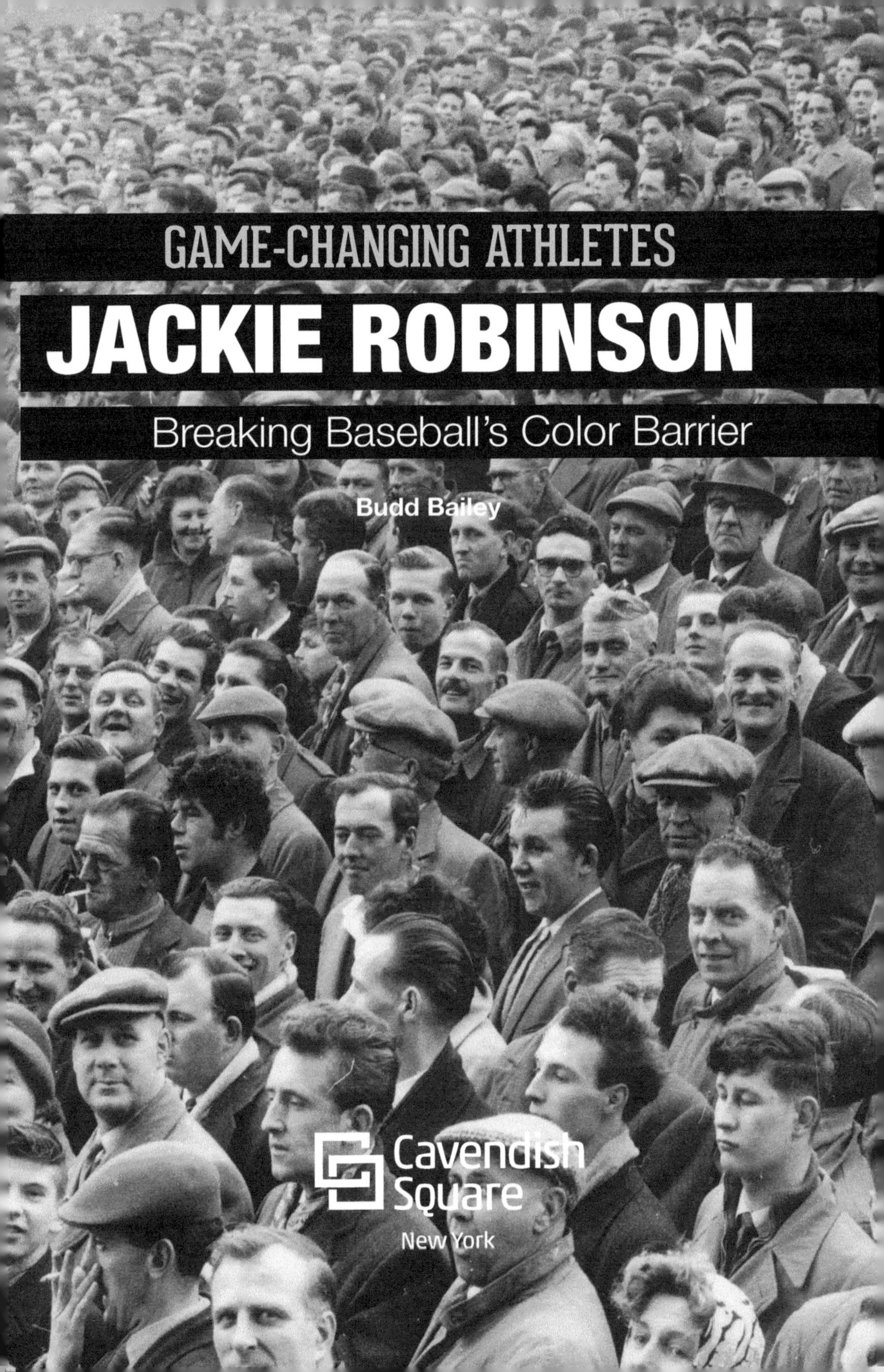

GAME-CHANGING ATHLETES

JACKIE ROBINSON

Breaking Baseball's Color Barrier

Budd Bailey

Cavendish Square
New York

Published in 2016 by Cavendish Square Publishing, LLC
243 5th Avenue, Suite 136, New York, NY 10016

First Edition

Cataloging-in-Publication Data

Names: Bailey, Budd, 1955-.
Title: Jackie Robinson: breaking baseball's color barrier / Budd Bailey.
Description: New York : Cavendish Square Publishing, 2016
| Series: Game-changing athletes | Includes index.
Identifiers: ISBN 9781502610560 (library bound) | ISBN 9781502610577 (ebook)
Subjects: LCSH: Robinson, Jackie, 1919-1972—Juvenile literature. | Baseball players—United States—Biography—Juvenile literature. | African American baseball players—Biography—Juvenile literature. | Discrimination in sports—United States—History—Juvenile literature.
Classification: LCC GV865.R6 B35 2016 | DDC 796.357'092—dc23

Editorial Director: David McNamara
Editor: Fletcher Doyle
Copy Editor: Rebecca Rohan
Art Director: Jeffrey Talbot
Designer: Joseph Macri
Senior Production Manager: Jennifer Ryder-Talbot
Production Editor: Renni Johnson
Photo Research: J8 Media

The photographs in this book are used by permission and through the courtesy of: Photo File/MLB Photos via Getty Images, cover; Keystone-France/Gamma Keystone via Getty Images, cover (background); Stephen Dunn/Getty Images, 5; Stephen Dunn/Getty Images,6; Hulton Archive/Getty Images, 8; AP Photo, 13, AP Photo/File, 17; Keystone/Getty Images, 20-21; Afro American Newspapers/Gado/Getty Images, 26; Sporting News via Getty Images, 28; Sporting News/Sporting News via Getty Images, 34; J. R. Eyerman/The LIFE Picture Collection/Getty Images, 41; AP Photo, 43; Nina Leen/The LIFE Picture Collection/Getty Images, 46; NY Daily News Archive via Getty Images, 48; Photo File/Getty Images, 52-53; Afro American Newspapers/Gado/Getty Images, 56; Andrew Burton/Getty Images, 59; William Greene/Sports Studio Photos/Getty Images, 63; Sporting News/Sporting News via Getty Images, 68; FPG/Archive Photos/Getty Images, 70; Hulton Archive/Getty Images, 78-79; AP Photo, 82; Focus on Sport/Getty Images, 84; MONICA M. DAVEY/AFP/Getty Images, 86; Afro American Newspapers/Gado/Getty Images, 88; Francis Miller/The LIFE Picture Collection/Getty Images, 95; Diamond Images/Getty Images, 98-99; Norman Potter/Express/Getty Images, background (used throughout).

Printed in the United States of America

CONTENTS

INTRODUCTION

The date was April 15, 2015, and the place was Dodger Stadium in Los Angeles. When the home team took the field that day, every player had "Dodgers" written across the front of his uniform, and a "42" on his back.

In other words, the players dressed the way Jackie Robinson had on April 15, 1947. What's more, the rest of the Dodgers and all of the opposing players wore 42 as well, and so did every team in every game in Major League Baseball that day. In fact, it's been a baseball tradition for every player in the league to wear the number 42 on April 15 for more than a decade.

Robinson became the first African American to play major league baseball in about sixty years when he took the field that day. Not only did he knock down a cultural wall, but he also took a large step toward the concept of equal rights for all Americans.

The proudest person on the Dodger Stadium field that day in 2015 might have been Jimmy Rollins. He had been traded to the Dodgers before the season began, so this was the first time he had taken part in Jackie Robinson Day as a member of the LA team. "The Dodgers and Branch Rickey had the courage to not only change baseball but also to help push America into the civil rights era, and Jackie had

Hall of Famer Sandy Koufax enjoys a moment with Rachel Robinson during the celebration of Jackie Robinson Day at Dodger Stadium in Los Angeles in 2015.

The chance to meet Jackie Robinson's widow had great significance for Jimmy Rollins, a member of the 2015 Dodgers.

the courage to not fight back against all the abuse he took," Rollins wrote in *Sports Illustrated*. "Sometimes I ask myself, could I have done that if I were in his shoes? I'm not sure. I do know that sacrifices that he made are a significant part of the reason why all African Americans, and Latin Americans too, can play the game today."

Looking back from today, it seems inevitable that blacks and whites would play baseball and other sports together. In reality, there was nothing inevitable about it. There had been essentially two kinds of Americas on the day the nation was founded—one white and one black—and it had stayed that way for 170 years. The divisions even extended to ballparks. In some stadiums, blacks could not even sit next to whites. Robinson represented a threat to that way of life. Remember, change can be scary. If he had failed to stay in the major leagues, who knows when another African American would have been allowed to try?

Luckily for all of us, Robinson was the right man in the right place at the right time. He quickly became one of the best baseball players in the major leagues, and eventually was voted into the National Baseball Hall of Fame in Cooperstown, New York. Before we knew it, equal opportunity came to baseball. Soon, many people realized that if it happened in baseball, it could happen in every part of society.

So as you read a story about how one man helped to change the lives of millions, think about Rollins' question. Could you have done what Jackie did?

The Robinson family traveled from Georgia to California in search of a better life. Jackie is second from the left.

CHAPTER 1

WEST COAST PREJUDICE

"A life is not important except in the impact it has on others."

—Jackie Robinson

Jackie Robinson's rise to fame might have been as unlikely as it was dramatic. Absolutely no one could have seen it coming.

Jack Robinson was born on January 31, 1919, on Hadley Ferry Road in Cairo, Georgia. The town is in the southwest corner of the state, 35 miles (56 kilometers) north of Tallahassee, Florida. Cairo is known to this day as "Syrup City," as **cane syrup** was produced there for almost all of the twentieth century. The high school's teams are known as the Syrupmakers, one of the unique team names in the nation. A few professional athletes have come out of Cairo in the past half-century, including Teresa Edwards. She played basketball for Team USA in five Olympic Games (winning four gold medals) after an All-American career at the University of Georgia.

Robinson was born less than a month after President Theodore Roosevelt died. Parents Jerry and Mallie Robinson gave their fifth child the middle name of Roosevelt in tribute. Jackie was the baby of the family, arriving after Edgar, Frank, Mack, and Willa Mae. When

Jackie was born, the family business was farming—to be specific, sharecropping.

When slavery came to an end after the Civil War, the former slaves in the South had few skills besides what they had learned while working on farms. Sharecropping was one of the few ways they could survive. Sharecropping was a system in which blacks—and poor whites—worked on land owned by someone else, and agreed to split the proceeds of crops with landlords or businesses that had provided necessary items such as seed or tools. Ideally, sharecroppers could save up a little money and buy land of their own at some point, but farming is by any standard an unreliable way of making a living, and many blacks went into debt because they couldn't pay for the use of tools and other supplies.

By the time Jackie Robinson was born, conditions for blacks had improved a little from the pre-Civil War horrors, but not much. Educational facilities for African Americans may have been separate, but they certainly weren't equal. The schools themselves were in bad shape, and supplies were either leftovers from the white schools or missing completely. What's more, blacks were still second-class citizens in a society controlled by whites.

What were the chances that a black child born in that environment would grow up to become one of the most significant figures in the twentieth century? They were very small. Less than a year later, the odds became microscopic.

Father Flees

Jackie's father Jerry had been working for $12 a month when he asked his boss for a raise. Since the landowner didn't want to lose him, he gave Jerry a new deal in which Jerry earned a larger share of the profits. It provided more money for the family, which was growing quickly; however, Jerry had been telling friends that he had become tired of farming. He said to Jackie's mother Mallie that he was going to visit his brother in Texas. Mallie was worried that Jerry wouldn't come back to Georgia after leaving, and she was right. That left Mallie and her five children to fend for themselves. Jackie later found out that his father had taken a neighbor's wife with him on the trip. Jackie and the rest of the children never saw their father again.

Georgia didn't have much to offer the Robinson family in 1920. The plantation owner was still angry with Mallie for urging Jerry to ask for more money, and the Robinsons were eventually ordered off the land. California, at least, offered a little hope. Mallie's brother Burton lived there, so the Robinsons packed up and moved to Pasadena, outside of Los Angeles. They landed in a city that was just starting to become famous as the setting for the annual Rose Bowl game on January 1. The college football contest had become a highlight of the city's calendar starting in 1916.

The Robinsons arrived in California when it was going through a boom in population. The transcontinental railroad had made the Golden State accessible to the masses, and thousands upon thousands made the trip over several decades in search of fortune. Chinese and Mexican workers came for jobs, even though the ones they could find were strenuous and difficult. Blacks also were the subject of **discrimination**.

Mallie did whatever she had to do in order to support her family. She took a series of jobs in order to make money and received **welfare**. The Robinsons got by on two meals a day, sometimes only because Mallie begged for a little extra food where she could find it.

Her children found out what discrimination, California-style, looked like. Only a few blacks lived in their neighborhood, and they received more than their share of harassment and threats. Rocks were thrown at the Robinson house, and a **cross** was burned on the lawn. The boys sometimes had to defend themselves with their fists, and they found themselves in trouble with the law every so often. One time Jackie and his friends were taken by gunpoint to see the sheriff. Their crime was that they had gone swimming in the reservoir. That was against the law in a society where blacks couldn't swim in public pools at the same time as whites. Mallie often had to come to the rescue and stick up for the rights of her children. You could say such incidents were training for what Jackie would encounter later in life.

When Jackie was about four years old, his mom was too busy working during the day to take care of him. Older sister Willa Mae took Jackie to her school, which let him play in the sandbox until school was dismissed. When it rained, Jackie was allowed to come inside and play in a classroom.

Mack Robinson (*right*) shown competing in the Los Angeles Coliseum, was an Olympic medalist in track.

Jackie graduated from Washington Junior High School in 1935 and was ready to move on to John Muir Technical High School. If there was any doubt about how he might spend some of his time after school was dismissed for the day, he had a pretty good role model in older brother Mack. Born in 1914, Mack attended Pasadena Junior College, where he set national records in track. That led to a trip to the 1936 Olympics, one of the most famous Games in history.

The Olympics that year were staged in Berlin, Germany. Those were the Games of Jesse Owens, who won an amazing four gold medals. Mack Robinson finished second in the 200-meter (218.7-yard) dash, falling four-tenths of a second short of earning a gold medal. That was pretty good for someone who once was told to give up athletics because of a heart condition.

No doubt inspired by his brother, Jackie had a spectacular athletic career at the mostly white Muir Tech. He turned out to be one of the best broad jumpers (now known as the long jump) in the region, collecting several awards. Robinson was the quarterback of the football team and a guard on the basketball team. On the baseball field, Robinson played shortstop and catcher. He was good enough to play in an all-star tournament in 1936. Jackie might not have noticed a couple of the others in that event, but he'd hear more about future baseball Hall of Famers Ted Williams and Bob Lemon down the road. Ted Williams played for the Boston Red Sox and was one of the best hitters in the game's history. Bob Lemon pitched for the Cleveland Indians and was named an all-star seven times.

Excelling in Everything

In that same year, Robinson showed he was good with a racket. He won the junior boys singles title in the Pacific Coast Negro Tennis Tournament. This is the same young man who picked up a ping-pong paddle at the age of fifteen and pronounced it a silly game. A few months later, he won the city championship—which put his name in a newspaper for the first time.

An athlete like that was bound to attract attention. The logical stop was the same as Mack's—Pasadena Junior College and its free tuition. Once again, Jackie was a one-man athletic department. He played shortstop and hit leadoff for the baseball team, and he was named the region's most valuable player (MVP) in addition to earning all-conference honors. On the track, Jackie broke the school long-jump record previously set by his brother Mack. He played guard for the basketball team and was the quarterback on the football team. On one memorable day, Robinson broke a school record in the long jump with a leap of 25 feet, 6.5 inches (7.8 meters). Then he got a ride to a Pasadena JC baseball game, just in time for the third inning. He entered the game, had two hits and two stolen bases, and helped his team win.

While on the football field, he suffered a broken ankle that kept him out of a few games as a freshman, but he finished the season as the first-team quarterback, and the following year he led Pasadena to eleven straight wins. Off the field, Robinson was selected to the Lancers, a campus group that patrolled school activities, and he was honored for his scholastic record and citizenship by the school.

Along the way, Jackie showed that he was ready to fight racism and discrimination without much prompting. When he protested the arrest of a black friend, Robinson himself was arrested. He earned a two-year suspended sentence and a reputation as a foe of injustice at a relatively young age. He must have been incensed when Mack could only land a low-level job for the city of Pasadena. He swept the streets in a USA Olympic jacket, his warmest coat. When a black sanitation worker won a court order to earn equal pay, all blacks—including Mack—lost their jobs. Mack is said to have later worked on a construction project at the Rose Bowl in Pasadena.

Robinson's performance at Pasadena created some interest from other universities, who were anxious to recruit him for the final two years of his education. While it's probable that Jackie never even considered going too far away from home because of the costs involved, the decision was made for him in a sense. His brother Frank was killed in a motorcycle accident, and Jackie was extremely close to him and the rest of his family. He decided to stay close to them, landing at the nearby University of California Los Angeles (UCLA).

Jackie Robinson was such a good athlete that he starred in another sport, football, at UCLA.

Big-time college football was barely integrated in 1939. Robinson was one of four blacks on the UCLA Bruins' roster that fall, and that made UCLA one of the most integrated in the nation. Robinson joined Kenny Washington and Woody Strode as part of the backfield. Washington was a second-team All-American selection. He played in a minor league of pro football in the early 1940s. When the Cleveland Rams of the National Football League moved to Los Angeles in 1946, they needed to have an integrated team in order to complete a lease agreement for a stadium. The Rams signed Washington in March 1946, making him the first African American to agree to a contract with an NFL team. He was later inducted into the College Football Hall of Fame.

Robinson, as usual, took part in other sports at UCLA. He was the NCAA champion in the broad jump, soaring 24 feet, 10.25 inches (7.6 m), and probably would have participated in the 1940 Olympics if they weren't canceled by World War II. Robinson also lettered in basketball and baseball, becoming the first Bruin to have that distinction in four different sports. In basketball, he led the Southern Division of the Pacific Coast Conference in scoring twice. His baseball stint was the least successful of the bunch, as his batting average was .097.

The Perfect Partner

While at UCLA, Robinson met the woman who eventually became his wife. Rachel Isum was a freshman, and Jackie's best friend, Ray Bartlett, introduced them. Rachel knew about Robinson's exploits on the sporting fields and courts in Westwood, and she first thought he was another stuck-up athlete. Soon he realized that Rachel was a very special young lady, and they fell in love. It was a surprise to her and Robinson's mother when he decided to drop out of college in the spring of 1941—falling just short of graduation. He just didn't know if education would help a black man get a good job in those times, and he wanted to see what he could find in the field of athletics.

Robinson took a job with a government agency in which he taught athletic skills to young people. When that program ended, he headed to Honolulu to play semi-professional football and to work in construction. Robinson returned to Los Angeles to sign with the Bulldogs of the Pacific Coast Football League—the same league that featured ex-teammate Washington. Jackie finished the season in November 1941 and left Hawaii on a ship on December 5. His timing was excellent. The surprise attack by Japanese forces on Pearl Harbor in Hawaii took place on December 7, 1941. It would be just a matter of time before millions of Americans would be wearing military uniforms.

Before leaving for the military, Robinson and pitcher Nate Moreland had a tryout with the Chicago White Sox in March 1942. It's easy to wonder what Jimmy Dykes, the manager of the White Sox, was thinking that day. He had managed a Chicago team that played an exhibition

Heavyweight champion Joe Louis joined the army during World War II and staged ninety-six boxing exhibitions to boost troop morale. He also advocated for more opportunities for, and better treatment of, African Americans in the military. He befriended Jackie Robinson and served as a role model for him.

game against the Pasadena Sox, a recreational team, in 1938. Dykes said after that game, "If that Robinson kid was white, I'd sign him right now. No one in the American League could make plays like that." Yet Robinson and Moreland were not offered contracts.

Robinson was shipped to Fort Riley in Kansas, one of the oldest military bases in the country. It was established in 1853, designed to protect settlers who were following trails across the Great Plains to points west. General George Armstrong Custer, later killed in the 1876 Battle of Little Bighorn against a confederation of Native American tribes, trained there. The battle in Montana came to be known as "**Custer's Last Stand**."

Robinson was well known enough at the time of his arrival at Fort Riley to be noted in stories in the Kansas City newspapers. During the summer of 1942, Robinson and some other blacks on the **segregated** base applied for the Officer Candidate School that was located at Fort Riley. They certainly were well qualified for such status, and the US Army had issued a regulation that skin color was not to be a factor in consideration for acceptance. Still, the process dragged on.

Robinson's situation changed because his name caught the attention of the most famous person at Fort Riley. It's difficult to imagine what sort of status Joe Louis had then in the African-American community. The boxer was the heavyweight champion of the world, and black America came to a standstill whenever he fought. Louis joined the

A MAN IN HIS CORNER

Joe Louis might have been the only person in America who had a good idea about what Jackie Robinson was going through at the start of his career. Louis got there first.

The boxer was born in 1914 in rural Alabama, moving to Detroit in 1926. He took up boxing in 1932 at the age of seventeen. Louis later turned pro and quickly climbed the ladder. There had been only one African-American heavyweight champion at that point (Jack Johnson, 1908–1915), but Louis overcame some prejudice and won the title in 1937. The win caused large celebrations in black communities.

Louis's finest moment came in 1938. He had already lost to Max Schmeling of Germany when they were both contenders in 1936. This time Louis was ready for a man promoted by Nazi Germany as an example of its superiority. All of America was rooting for Louis under these circumstances, and he delivered a knockout in two minutes, four seconds in the first round.

Louis went through a string of opponents easily, joined the US Army and met Robinson in Kansas, and went back to boxing after the war. Louis retired in 1949 as champion, but financial pressures forced him back into the ring after his skills had faded. Louis's career ended in 1951 when he was knocked out by future heavyweight champion Rocky Marciano. Louis was a world heavyweight champion for almost twelve years, which is still a record. He died in 1981.

"I'm sure if it wasn't for Joe Louis, the **color line** in baseball would not have been broken for another ten years," Robinson said.

military once World War II started and fought exhibition bouts before the troops.

It was Robinson's good fortune to be on the same base as Louis. When the champ heard about the situation involving Robinson, Louis told others that he wasn't happy. Shortly after that, Robinson and his friends were accepted into OCS. What's more, the incident led to a long-term friendship between Robinson and Louis.

Robinson became a second lieutenant in January 1943 and celebrated by becoming engaged to Rachel. The couple did have ups and downs in their relationship due to the distance between them, as she was back in California. Robinson was transferred to Fort Hood, Texas, which was located north of Austin and was named after a Confederate general. There, he joined a tank battalion. While on leave, he frequently visited a nearby old friend, Reverend Karl Downs, the president of Samuel Houston College. Rev. Downs had been Robinson's pastor in Pasadena.

By 1944, Robinson's military career must have seemed uneventful by many standards. Perhaps central Texas wasn't the ideal location for a young black man who wasn't used to the South, but it was safe from the bombing and shooting of war. He was used to army discrimination somewhat by then. Robinson had tried out for the baseball team at Fort Hood and was told by the white officer who coached the team, "You have to play for the colored team." There was no colored team. Still, he was caught off guard by what happened on July 6, 1944, when Robinson went through a personal nightmare that no doubt influenced his view of his country.

Military Injustice

That day, Robinson got on a bus and sat next to a fellow officer's wife, an African American who was light skinned and to many looked white. The US Army had its own bus line, and it was desegregated. Still, Robinson was told by the driver to move to the back of the bus. In a letter to Truman K. Gibson, the Assistant to the Secretary of War, Robinson wrote, "It is evident that the driver seemed to resent my talking to her and told me to move to the rear. He didn't ask the lady to move so I refused." Robinson explained his point of view in his autobiography, *I Never Had It Made*.

"I was aware of the fact that recently Joe Louis and Ray Robinson had refused to move to the backs of buses in the South," he wrote. "The resulting publicity had caused the Army to put out regulations barring racial discrimination on any vehicle operating on an Army post. Knowing about these regulations, I had no intention of being intimidated into moving to the back of the bus."

The driver didn't take immediate action, but at the end of the trip he called the military police. Robinson was taken into custody. When the questioning over the incident started to take a racist tone, Robinson complained. That earned him a recommendation of a **court-martial**. Robinson's commander wouldn't take the next legal step in the process, instead

Jackie Robinson found his days in the armed forces to be difficult.

transferring him to another battalion. However, the commander there opted to charge Robinson with a variety of offenses, including public drunkenness. That was a surprise to Robinson, who didn't drink.

The court-martial took place in August 1944, and the story had received wide publicity in what was called the black press—newspapers that were produced in big cities but which were read by African Americans all across the country. They found out that the charges against Robinson had been reduced to a couple of counts of insubordination during questioning. Even those didn't stick, as Robinson was acquitted by a nine-man panel of white officers. What's more, the legal proceedings caused him to miss his deployment to the European theater, so he never did see combat duty during the war. His unit fought enemy forces for 183 straight days in six different countries in some of the most difficult action of that period, including the **Battle of the Bulge**.

Certainly Robinson learned a few lessons about the state of race relations during the entire episode. While black and white soldiers all fought the same enemy, racism within the military's ranks was very present. However, Robinson had fought injustice, with determination and dignity, and won. He probably learned a few things along the way, and one of them was that he didn't feel comfortable serving in the Armed Forces anymore.

After his acquittal, Robinson was transferred to Camp Breckinridge in Kentucky. There he was a coach in an athletic program. Robinson received an honorable discharge in November 1944. Even so, he was not awarded veterans' benefits upon that departure.

Before he left the army, he made a friendship that had a long-lasting effect on his life and the country. Robinson encountered Ted Alexander, a member of the Kansas City Monarchs of the Negro American League in baseball. He urged Robinson to send a letter to Thomas Baird, the team's co-owner, asking for a tryout. Robinson did so. Maybe he thought it was like entering the lottery. Who knew where it could lead and what could happen?

Jackie Robinson started his professional baseball career with the Kansas City Monarchs of the Negro Leagues.

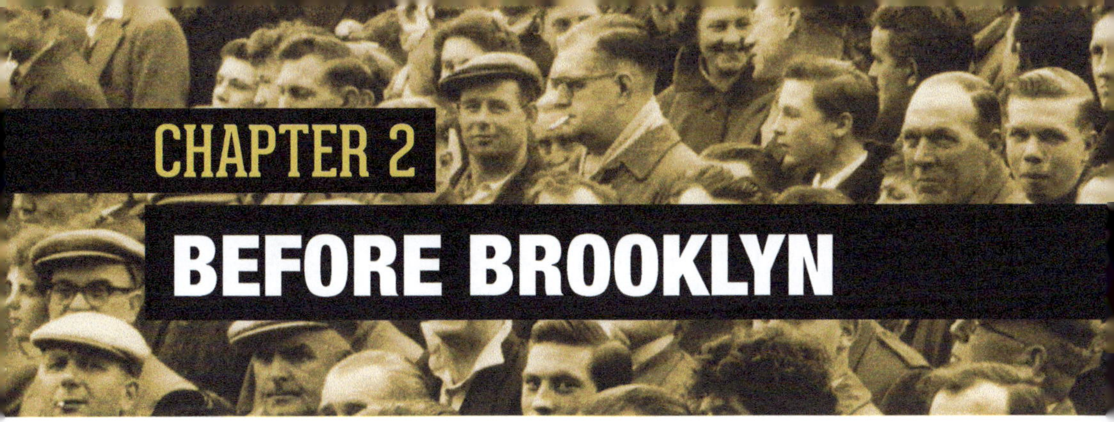

CHAPTER 2

BEFORE BROOKLYN

"I'm not concerned with your liking or disliking me ... All I ask is that you respect me as a human being."

—Jackie Robinson

If Jackie Robinson didn't have an idea what he was going to do once he had finished his service in the military, he had a lot of company. He just arrived at that point early because of his discharge in 1944. World War II lasted until the summer of 1945. Millions of American servicemen were about to enter a world that was different than the one in which they had lived before December 7, 1941.

After about sixteen years of economic depression and war, the nation was ready to get back to "normal." Millions of men came home from overseas, found jobs, got married, bought homes, and had children. Much of the rest of the world was literally in ruins, leaving the United States as the world's most powerful nation. An economic boom in America was right around the corner.

Speaking of a different world, African Americans were more than ready for that. During the war, President Franklin Roosevelt had signed a bill that ordered companies involved in federal projects to have a fully integrated workforce. Blacks were given new responsibilities—and they thrived in them. They also knew that the **GI Bill** had been passed to pay for educational opportunities for all soldiers.

Yet attitudes and beliefs weren't so quick to change. Segregation was the still the way of life in many places. It was particularly true in the South, where Jim Crow laws—government rules permitting segregation and discrimination that lasted for a century—weren't going to go away easily. Still, more and more black people were wondering why they couldn't live better and more equal lives. Robinson was one of them.

When Robinson first began looking for work, athletics was a logical starting point. He played football with his old team, the Los Angeles Bulldogs, briefly. But then his longtime friend from Pasadena, Rev. Karl Downs, offered him the athletic director's job at Sam Houston College in Austin, Texas. Jackie took the position and did a good job.

Robinson didn't stay in Austin for long. In 1945, he received a baseball contract offer from the Kansas City Monarchs of the Negro Leagues. Hilton Smith of the Monarchs, himself a future Hall of Famer, had urged team owner J. L. Wilkinson to sign Robinson. At twenty-six, Jackie was ready to try his luck at professional athletics, and this was the logical place.

Line Is Drawn

Blacks had played baseball since the sport grew in popularity after the conclusion of the Civil War. Their participation in organized leagues was sometimes limited by prejudice and league rules. All-white teams often refused to take the field against an opponent with a black player. The number of blacks in the professional leagues decreased until they disappeared by the late 1880s.

Negro leagues came on the scene once a "color line" was drawn, but they were small-time operations. That changed in 1920. Rube Foster had been talking about an all-black league with black ownership for several years, and after the end of World War I, he started the National Association of Colored Professional Baseball Clubs. It would be difficult to say the league thrived, but the number of teams grew and a World Series was held to determine a champion in 1924. Some of the greatest names in the history of the sport—Satchel Paige, Josh Gibson, and Oscar Charleston—played for those teams.

The Negro Leagues weren't well organized at any point in their history, and statistics about those days aren't complete. Even so, Robinson was a smash hit as a rookie baseball player. According to baseball-reference.com, he hit .414 in sixty-three at-bats and played in the 1945 Negro League All-Star Game.

Still, Robinson had bigger dreams. He wasn't too happy about the lack of structure, difficult travel, or frequent gambling that surrounded the Negro Leagues. Robinson later said that he probably would have given up baseball after the 1945 season if he didn't have the chance to move to the major leagues. He might have returned to college coaching instead.

In an attempt to take that step, Robinson accepted an invitation to try out with the Boston Red Sox of the American League in April 1945. He and two other members of the Negro Leagues—Sam Jethroe and Marvin Williams—went to Fenway Park on the eve of the season. Isadore Muchnick, a Boston city councilman, had applied pressure on the Red Sox to give blacks a chance to join the team. Robinson said later, "We knew we were wasting our time," but he thought he could help the cause of advancement for black players. A reporter who watched the ninety-minute workout said a voice coming from the team offices ordered the black players off the field in no uncertain terms, with a racial slur added for emphasis. After smashing baseballs all around Fenway Park, Robinson and the others were essentially told, "Don't call us. We'll call you." The Red Sox didn't call. The team was the last of the major league clubs to integrate (1959). Robinson carried hard feelings toward the Red Sox with him for the rest of his life.

While Boston's interest in black players was less than genuine, another team had been quietly investigating that idea. General Manager Branch Rickey of the Brooklyn Dodgers was getting ready to take that leap, a subject that had been on his mind for quite a while.

Rickey's initial thought on the subject came in 1910 when he was a coach for Ohio Wesleyan University. The team had a black player, Charley Thomas, who stayed on a cot in Rickey's room on a road trip after the hotel owner had refused to give Thomas a regular room. He started sobbing about his hands, saying, "If only they were white, I'd be as good as anybody then, wouldn't I, Mr. Rickey?" Rickey never forgot the incident.

Rickey later moved into the front office of the St. Louis Cardinals. He quickly established a reputation as one of the most creative thinkers in baseball history, as he brought several new ideas to the sport. St. Louis won four World Series titles during his time there. In 1942, Rickey was hired to run the Dodgers. It took him a year to ask the team's board of directors for permission to start scouting black players.

Scaling a Mountain

The chance that a black man would be allowed to play in organized baseball grew in 1944, when Commissioner Kenesaw Mountain Landis died. Landis had taken over that job in 1920. The record concerning Landis's views on the subject of integration are mixed. His public statements pointed out that there was no rule against blacks playing organized baseball, which was true. However, one minor-league owner said he was told by Landis privately that if he went ahead with an integration plan in 1939, he would be banned from baseball for life. Landis later reportedly told the Pittsburgh Pirates not to sign slugger Josh Gibson. Most of the sport's owners were against integration—some were making money by renting their stadiums to Negro League teams—and Landis didn't do anything to change the situation.

Landis was replaced as commissioner in 1945 by Albert "Happy" Chandler, a former US senator and governor of Kentucky. Chandler was much more open to the idea of allowing blacks into the game. In addition, New York City was home to many political groups in 1945, and many wanted the color line in baseball broken. They put pressure on the New York teams to do something.

Rickey announced in 1945 that he and the Dodgers were starting a new Negro league called the United States League, and a team named the Brooklyn Brown Dodgers would be part of it. Thus the team's scouts were free to look for black talent without attracting much attention. Rickey later admitted that the story was a smokescreen designed to mask his true intentions.

Dodger scouts crossed the country looking for top players, and Robinson quickly caught their eyes with his

Jackie Robinson and Dodgers executive Branch Rickey developed a warm relationship while the two men were together in Brooklyn.

THE BLACK BABE RUTH

If Brooklyn Dodgers general manager Branch Rickey had been looking in 1945 for simply the best black player to add to his team's roster, he probably wouldn't have picked Jackie Robinson. Rickey might have picked a catcher named Josh Gibson. That's because Gibson is considered one of the greatest catchers in baseball history and one of the best hitters of all time.

Gibson broke into the Negro Leagues at the age of eighteen, and he played there and for a couple of leagues outside of the United States during his career. Statistics about his play are rather sketchy, and the quality of the opponents—which included exhibition games—was uneven. Even so, some have estimated that Gibson hit more than eight hundred homers. Some called him "the black Babe Ruth," while others said Ruth was "the white Josh Gibson." Buck O'Neil, who played against Gibson for ten years in the Negro Leagues, compared him to a more modern slugger in 1999: "When you watch Mark McGwire hit a home run, you're watching Josh Gibson."

Hitting is all about timing, but Josh's timing away from the ballpark wasn't good. He was born a few years too early to compete with all of the best players in baseball. Gibson was diagnosed with a brain tumor in 1943, and he developed a drug problem and suffered from depression. Yet he kept on playing until he died at the age of thirty-five of a stroke in Pittsburgh in 1947—only three months after Robinson made his major league debut.

The Baseball Hall of Fame started to induct the best players from the Negro Leagues in 1971. Gibson went in with Buck Leonard in the second class. He was enshrined the year after the legendary Satchel Paige.

play. The rookie was still relatively young and had shown character and intelligence throughout his adult life. Robinson had attended college and played on integrated teams in the past. Much to the delight of the pious Rickey, Robinson did not drink or smoke. Some of the other top black baseball players had not returned from World War II yet, while Robinson had been discharged and thus was available right away. Chief scout Clyde Sukeforth went to Chicago to invite Robinson to come to Brooklyn for a meeting with Rickey. The chat was held at the Dodgers' offices on August 28, 1945, and it turned into a session lasting more than two hours.

Robinson was stunned to hear that Rickey didn't want him for the Brown Dodgers; he wanted him in the Brooklyn Dodgers organization. Rickey made sure that Robinson knew what he was getting into. He told him about the taunts, insults, and slurs that certainly would come his way from fans on the road, even testing him with sample remarks. Rickey no doubt brought up the fact that Robinson would be a target from opposing players. Not only would they scream at him, but pitchers would intentionally hit him with the ball at the plate and runners would spike him on the field. Umpires might call him out when he was safe.

At one point in the interview, Rickey told Jackie that he would have to take all of this abuse without responding. The Dodgers' executive was worried that such a response might damage the chances of Robinson making the transition successfully, especially in light of Robinson's history of fighting such attitudes earlier in the life. Robinson was shocked: "Are you looking for a Negro who is afraid to fight back?" Rickey replied he was looking for someone "with guts enough not to fight back." Robinson agreed to that condition.

The two sides agreed to a contract. The catch was that Robinson couldn't tell anyone about it yet. Rickey planned to announce it in public by November 1, 1945. Robinson left the Monarchs and went home. There was some talk that Rickey planned to announce the signing of several black players at once, but that didn't happen.

A Major Announcement

On October 23, a little ahead of schedule, the Dodgers called a news conference and announced that Robinson had signed a contract to play with the Montreal Royals of the International League, Brooklyn's top minor-league affiliate. He would be the first African American to play in that league since the 1880s. Robinson later told reporters about that time, "I'm ready to take the chance. Maybe I'm doing something for my race."

The announcement must have been stunning to all Americans. It wasn't just a sports story. It was news that affected society as a whole. Reaction was swift. A *New York Daily News* writer rated Robinson's chances of success at a thousand to one—even though he had never seen him play. A *Sporting News* editorial said Robinson would never make

SCORECARD

Hitting: Career .311 average, with a major league best .342 in 1949, and 137 home runs.

Fielding: Holds record for best fielding percentage among second basemen who played at least 150 games, with a .992 mark; holds record for most double plays by a second baseman with 137 in 1951; led second basemen in double plays 1949–1952.

Running: Stole 197 bases, leading league with twenty-nine in 1947 and thirty-seven in 1949.

All-Star: Named a National League All-Star six straight seasons, 1949–1954, earning game MVP in 1949.

World Series: Played in six World Series with the Brooklyn Dodgers, batting .234, with one title in 1955.

Other Awards: Congressional Gold Medal; Presidential Medal of Freedom; First African American inducted into the Baseball Hall of Fame, in 1962; inducted into UCLA Hall of Fame; first baseball player depicted on a US postage stamp; has NL rookie of the year award named in his honor; has baseball stadium at UCLA dedicated in his honor.

it in Triple-A baseball, let alone the majors. Interestingly, some criticism came from members of the Negro Leagues. While there was little doubt that Robinson was a good player, he wasn't an all-time great yet. That distinction went to such players as Gibson and Paige. Larry Doby, future Cleveland Indian, suggested later that Gibson, a home-run-hitting catcher, was so disappointed not to be signed first that he died at a young age of a broken heart. Paige, the great pitcher, took the news with grace: "They didn't make a mistake by signing Robinson. They couldn't have picked a better one."

Even Robinson's allies knew what he was approaching. Sportswriter Wendell Smith, the leading black baseball journalist of his time, wrote in December 1945 that Robinson had "the hopes, aspirations and ambitions of thirteen million black Americans heaped upon his broad, sturdy shoulders."

Robinson had started to tune up for his new life as soon as he signed the contract. He played with a team in the California Winter League, and then toured South America. Robinson capped the busy offseason in February 1946, when he married fiancée Rachel Isum.

Soon after the wedding, the Robinsons headed to spring training in Daytona Beach, Florida. If Jackie didn't know how difficult his new job would be, he found out quickly. He and Rachel tried to fly to Florida, but they were bumped off flights in favor of whites and weren't allowed to eat in restaurants. They switched to a bus for the final part of the trip. Upon arrival, these two California residents were shocked to see signs on public facilities that read "whites only." Even Jackie's manager wasn't on his side at the start. Clay Hopper, who was from Mississippi, had asked that Robinson be placed with any team but Montreal in the Dodgers' farm system. Hopper reportedly told Rickey that he would have to move his family out of Mississippi if he managed a black ballplayer. The request was denied.

Florida was a much different place then than it is now. Much of the state resembled the rest of the Old South, an area that was decidedly inhospitable toward blacks. When Robinson first arrived in Daytona Beach, he was told that he couldn't live with the rest of his new white teammates. Instead, Jackie roomed with a local black politician.

At least Robinson had a little company on the Montreal roster. Pitcher Johnny Wright, an African American, had been signed by the Dodgers in January 1946. Wright was twenty-nine when he joined the Dodgers at Daytona Beach. When those two walked on the practice field for the first time, they knocked down a barrier in the process.

Locked Doors

The pressure on Robinson must have been beyond belief. The police chief in Sanford, where the Royals worked out with another Brooklyn minor-league team, threatened to cancel games if Robinson was allowed to play; Jackie went back to Daytona Beach. There was talk that some people in Sanford had organized a mob that intended to

Blacks and whites couldn't play on the same field in several parts of the country in the first half of the twentieth century.

lynch Jackie and Rachel, who were whisked out of town. The Royals found the Jacksonville stadium padlocked on the day they were scheduled to play there. In Deland, a day game was called off—supposedly because of faulty lighting. Opposing pitchers frequently hit Robinson with pitches. Through it all, Jackie relied on the companionship and love of Rachel, as they took things one day at a time in what they knew was going to be a long process.

Still, there were some good moments. Rickey convinced the civic leaders of Daytona Beach to host a game between the Royals and the Dodgers, who were training in Jacksonville. Robinson was in the Montreal lineup on March 17, 1946. It was another big step, as Robinson became the first black man to play in a game involving teams in organized ball in more than a half-century.

The Dodgers eventually decided that Robinson would be a better fit at second base than at shortstop, so he was moved late in training camp to that position. That's where he played when he made his debut for Montreal on April 18, 1946. The site was Roosevelt Stadium in Jersey City, New Jersey, and Game One turned out to be quite dramatic.

A sportswriter called the game "another Emancipation Day." Rachel couldn't sit still, so she walked around the stands to ease the tension a bit. Jackie didn't even look at the stands, out of fear that only African Americans would be applauding him, but when he stood for the

Robinson receives congratulations from teammate George Shuba after hitting his first home run with Montreal.

national anthem, he realized it all really was happening and considered it "a day of destiny."

The starting pitcher for Jersey City was Warren Sandel, who had played against Robinson when they both lived in California. Before Robinson's first at-bat, catcher Dick Bouknight demanded that Sandel throw the ball at Robinson, but the pitcher refused. On a 3–2 pitch, Robinson grounded out to shortstop. But that was the last time for the day that Jersey City could retire Robinson. He homered in his next at-bat, earning a pat on the back from Hopper as Jackie rounded third. When Robinson crossed the plate, he was greeted by teammate George Shuba. "You could see it in his face, how happy he was," Shuba said. "You could see he was just overwhelmed with joy."

In his next at-bat, Robinson reached base on a bunt single, stole second, moved to third on a ground out, and then scored on a **balk**. For those who thought that scoring a run that way was a fluke, Robinson so unnerved a pitcher in the eighth inning that he too balked him home.

Robinson finished the day with four hits in a 14–1 win. The sellout crowd surrounded Robinson after the game. "I couldn't have dreamed up a better start," Robinson said. After the game, Rachel said to Jackie, "Little man, you've had a busy day."

Feeling Welcome

Robinson felt a little bruised, mentally and physically, after a spring training session in the South and the opening road trip to Jersey City and Baltimore. But Montreal was different, much different. The community welcomed both Robinsons with open arms. Rachel said later she couldn't remember a single incident there that year. She said to Jackie, "How can a few miles, a mere border, make that much of a difference in people?"

The road trips were different. Jackie took all sorts of abuse from fans and opponents. One time in Syracuse, a player threw a black cat out of the dugout and on the field. Then he said, "Hey, Robinson, here's your cousin." But wherever Robinson went, he attracted interest and filled ballparks. More than one million fans saw him play that season, an amazing number at the time for minor-league baseball.

Jackie was lucky enough to have Rachel with him during that difficult season. She impressed everyone who met her as a person of class, dignity, and intelligence. Minor-league general manager Buzzie Bavasi once sat near her at a game in Montreal and watched all of the other Royals' wives talk to her. Rickey later asked Bavasi if Jackie was a good enough person to play for the Dodgers. Bavasi is said to have answered, "If Jack Roosevelt Robinson is good enough for Rachel, he's good enough for us."

The rest of the major-league teams were watching what was happening in the minors, and many executives weren't happy about it. In August, several major-league owners expressed concerns that having blacks on their teams might lessen the value of their franchises. They had fears that if the black population turned out for games, white people

The Robinson family was treated with warmth during its year in Montreal in 1946.

might simply stay home. But Commissioner Chandler was on Rickey's side, and that made a huge difference.

Robinson certainly showed he could play at the highest minor-league level in 1946. He hit .349, stole forty bases, scored a league-high 113 runs, and had a .985 fielding percentage—all while coping with enough pressure to push him close to a nervous breakdown. Montreal ran away with the regular season title and beat the Newark Bears in the International League championship series, four games to one. One of the most memorable days in Robinson's career came at the very end of the season, in the Little World Series against the champion of the American Association. After the last game in Montreal, in which the Royals defeated the Louisville Colonels for the title, Hopper said to him, "It's been an honor to be your manager, Jackie. You are a complete ballplayer and a real gentleman."

Then Robinson was mobbed by adoring fans. He had to catch a plane to Detroit, so he eventually had to run away from the crowd. Writer Sam Maltin wrote, "It was probably the only day in history that a black man ran from a white mob with love, instead of lynching, on its mind."

Brooklyn manager Leo Durocher thought Jackie Robinson could help the Dodgers win.

CHAPTER 3

1947

"We knew the end goal was important. We weren't going to lose because some crazies were shouting insults and throwing balls at his head."

—Rachel Robinson

In the spring of 1947, baseball's record book said that only three African Americans had ever played in the major leagues. Bill White of Providence came first in 1879, and brothers Moses Fleetwood Walker and Welday Walker were members of the Toledo Blue Stockings of 1884. Jackie Robinson hoped to be the fourth in 1947. As you'd expect, it took some effort to get him there and keep him there.

The Dodgers had four other black players in the organization by the time spring training opened in 1947: Roy Campanella, Don Newcombe, John Wright, and Roy Partlow. Daytona Beach had shown that hosting an integrated team in Florida came with problems, so team executive Branch Rickey took his entire organization to another country. The Dodgers trained in Havana, Cuba.

Those four players were reminded that baseball was filled with Southern natives who held the region's racist views. There were some whites who hated blacks just because they were black, and others who had never been exposed to blacks on a daily basis. Outfielder Dixie Walker sent a letter to Rickey that spring asking to be traded without mentioning Robinson by name. He also was involved in starting a petition urging the Dodgers not to place Robinson on the roster. Walker later said that he did it because he wasn't sure how his family and business would fare in Alabama once it was known that he had a black man as a teammate.

The Brooklyn manager at the start of training camp was one of the legendary characters in baseball history, Leo Durocher. He had been a loud infielder for close to twenty years in the majors and was just as loud as a manager. Durocher was a man who would do almost anything to win and who had trouble with the authority figures in his life. If nothing else, though, Durocher set the tone for Robinson's attempt to make the major league team during spring training. He made his feelings very clear with a speech after he heard about a player revolt over Robinson's presence: "I do not care if the guy is yellow or black, or if he has stripes like a … zebra. I'm the manager of this team, and I say he plays. What's more, I say he can make us all rich. And if any of you cannot use the money, I will see that you are all traded."

However, Durocher didn't manage the Dodgers for a day of the 1947 regular season. Baseball commissioner Happy Chandler suspended him for a year on April 9 for "association with known gamblers." If Robinson wondered what effect the suspension would have on him, the answers came quickly, and they were supportive. The next day, the

Dodgers bought Robinson's contract from the Montreal Royals, which meant he had made the team. The Dodgers also named Burt Shotton as the interim manager for 1947. Shotton had been a friend of Rickey's for more than thirty years and was extremely loyal to him.

Putting on a Show

Robinson had made his case earlier in spring training during a seven-game series between Brooklyn and Montreal that was played in Panama. Rickey had told Robinson to make as much of an impact as a player as possible in that series. Jackie followed orders with a sensational week in which he hit .625. Now he was officially a Dodger, and Robinson tuned up for the regular season during a three-game preseason series against the New York Yankees. He drove in five runs and fielded his position flawlessly.

April 15, 1947, was opening day for the Dodgers, as Brooklyn hosted the Boston Braves at Ebbets Field. Jackie told Rachel on his way out the door that morning, "Just in case you have trouble picking me out, I'll be wearing number 42." A crowd of 26,623 watched the game, with more blacks than whites in the stands. They saw Robinson take the field with his teammates for the top of the first inning, and a color line that was about sixty years old was shattered. On one of Joe Hatten's first pitches of the day, Dick Culler of the Braves hit a ground ball to Spider Jorgensen at third. Jorgensen threw to Robinson at first, and umpire Al Barlick called Culler out.

Brooklyn Dodgers Spider Jorgensen, Pee Wee Reese, Eddie Stanky, and Jackie Robinson are ready for Opening Day in 1947.

Dodgers
Dodgers
Dodgers

In the bottom of the first inning, Eddie Stanky led off for the Dodgers with a ground out. Next up was Robinson, facing Johnny Sain. It would have been nice for history's sake for Robinson to have gotten a hit in that situation. Instead, Robinson hit a weak grounder to third, and Bob Elliott of the Braves threw him out. In the bottom of the third, Robinson flew out to Danny Litwhiler in left field. Later, Robinson received a lesson in the skills of the major leaguers. What looked like a sure hit was turned into a sparkling double play by Culler, the Braves' shortstop.

Robinson made an impact on the game with his feet in the seventh inning. The Dodgers trailed the Braves, 3–2, and Stanky was on first after a walk. Robinson placed a bunt down the first-base line. First baseman Earl Torgeson knew he had to hurry after fielding the ball, and his throw hit Robinson on the base line. The ball bounced away, and when it was retrieved, Robinson was on second and Stanky was on third. That brought up Pete Reiser, who doubled home both runners to give the Dodgers the lead. Reiser later scored on a sacrifice fly.

When Brooklyn took the field for the top of the ninth, Robinson stayed in the dugout. Howie Schultz came in as a defensive replacement as Shotton switched to someone with more experience at the position. Relief pitcher Hugh Casey preserved the lead, and the Dodgers walked off the field with a 5–3 win. Robinson had gone 0 for 3 with a sacrifice and scored the winning run.

The newspapers barely mentioned Robinson in their stories the next day, as Reiser's play was featured. Columnist Arthur Daley of the *New York Times* said Robinson's debut was "uneventful." That's not the word that would come to mind in hindsight. America and its national pastime had become a different place in a single afternoon.

Three days later, Robinson hit his first major-league homer at the Polo Grounds in New York against the Giants. Blacks who rooted for the Giants said they had mixed emotions. "We said, 'Oh, Lord, don't let him strike out,'" said Colin Powell, the future secretary of state who was then a ten-year-old living in the Bronx.

Jeering Section

It didn't take long for Robinson to find out what he'd face from opponents. Later in April, the Philadelphia Phillies came to Ebbets Field for a three-game series. The Phillies were managed by Ben Chapman, who spent most of his non-baseball life in Alabama. Baseball players of that era weren't known for being polite, and insults were often shouted from the dugouts. But when the Phillies saw Robinson, they turned up the venom several notches. So many racial slurs and insults were tossed at Robinson that it became a major news story. Chapman at one point suggested that Robinson should "go back to the cotton fields." Some of the Phillies made gestures like snipers, pointing their bats like guns at Robinson. The abuse reached the point where

Jackie Robinson agreed to pose for a photo with Philadelphia manager Ben Chapman, in spite of Chapman's racial abuse during games.

Stanky—who was from Alabama—asked Chapman why he didn't pick on someone who could fight back.

Robinson didn't have a great series, going 3 for 12 without an extra-base hit. But the Dodgers did better, sweeping the series as they allowed a total of two runs in the three games. Rickey later said Chapman did a great job of uniting the Dodgers, to the point where it was "us versus them." It was all part of a good start for Brooklyn. The Dodgers won the first eight of their home games and ten of the first eleven. Brooklyn was in first place at the end of April, a spot they would hold for much of the season. Robinson was slumping by the end of his first month, and some wondered if it was time for him to sit for a game or two. Off the field, though, he was an instant star and a fan favorite. His phone kept ringing, and he was invited to dozens of public functions.

The next bit of drama came in May. The Dodgers had a long road trip scheduled that would take them through five cities. The first stop was in Philadelphia. Phillies general manager Herb Pennock suggested that the Dodgers shouldn't bring Robinson to town because Philadelphia wasn't ready for it. Rickey said he'd be delighted to accept the forfeits, and Pennock backed down. Then, when the Dodgers checked in at the Benjamin Franklin Hotel in Philadelphia, they were told that they shouldn't return if they had any Negroes. The Dodgers moved to the Warwick Hotel, but Robinson felt disappointment for making his team feel like outcasts.

In Pittsburgh, Robinson reached first base with a hit. The Pittsburgh first baseman was Hank Greenberg. Not

BASEBALL'S LITTLE BIG MAN

Harold "Pee Wee" Reese was coming home from World War II in October 1945, on a boat in the Pacific Ocean, when a shipmate delivered some big news. The Brooklyn Dodgers had signed a black player. Then came the punch line. "He's a shortstop," the shipmate added.

Reese, who stood five foot, ten inches (1.8 m) and weighed only 160 pounds (76.2 kilograms), had been the starter at that position for the Dodgers in 1941 and 1942. Then it was off to the war. Reese thought about it for a while and came to the conclusion that if this new Dodger was good enough to win his job, then he was entitled to take it. But it did cross his mind that some people back in his native Louisville, Kentucky, might not be happy if he lost his starting spot to a black man.

Thankfully, Reese didn't have to worry about losing his job. By 1947, he and Robinson were both starters in the Dodger infield.

During the course of spring training in 1947, some of the Dodgers started a petition to have Robinson removed from the roster. A few players—mostly Southerners—signed it. Reese was asked to do so but did not. He told sportswriter Roger Kahn much later that he didn't feel he had the right to deny Robinson the chance to earn a livelihood. However, he admitted that he didn't want to put it to his teammates quite that way. So Reese said that he was afraid the plan would backfire, and that he'd be out of work. With a wife and a family, he couldn't afford that.

Reese and Robinson eventually became more than just teammates. Their relationship was best shown by an incident that has become famous over the years as an example of brotherhood and respect. According to the story, Robinson was the target of heckling from fans in Cincinnati during his first season in the major leagues. At some point, Reese came over to Robinson and put his arm around him in support. The crowd immediately turned quiet.

Brooklyn won't forget the friendship between Jackie Robinson and Pee Wee Reese, thanks to this statue.

As Robinson's fame grew over the years, so did the impact of the incident. Many people said they saw it happen, but some remembered it in Boston instead of Cincinnati, and some remembered it in 1948 instead of 1947. Perhaps the confusion comes with the fact that Robinson said it happened more than once.

In 2005, a statue of the two men, with Reese's arm around Robinson, was unveiled outside of the stadium of the Brooklyn Cyclones, a minor-league team. "It's a historic symbol of a wonderful legacy of friendship, teamwork, of courage—of a lot of things we hope we will be able to pass on to young people," Rachel Robinson said at the dedication ceremony.

Reese was a ten-time All-Star and was inducted into the Hall of Fame in 1984. After a long illness, he died in 1999.

only was Greenberg was one of the game's great sluggers, but he was also the most prominent player of the Jewish faith in the game. Greenberg knew something about abuse from fans. "Stick in there. You're doing fine. Keep your chin up," Greenberg said to Robinson, who said after the game, "Class sticks out all over Mr. Greenberg." While in Pittsburgh, the Dodgers called a players-only meeting that excluded Robinson. Organizer and pitcher Ralph Branca told his teammates, "We have to get behind Jackie to help him. They're all on him. He's gonna be here. He's here to stay. And he's going to help us win the **pennant**."

It was on to Chicago, where the Cubs were said to have thrown something at Robinson every time he stepped in the batter's box. At one of those games, a twelve-year-old named Allan "Bud" Selig sat in the stands. As an adult, he became the owner of the Milwaukee Brewers and then baseball commissioner.

Boycott Squashed

The trip concluded in St. Louis. If you made a map of where major league baseball teams were located in 1947, St. Louis was the farthest south and the farthest west. That city and Cincinnati probably carried attitudes that were closest to those in the South. There were rumors circulating well before that trip that the St. Louis players were planning to organize a boycott in protest to Robinson's presence. Not only would the Cardinals not take the field, but the other teams would not play that day either. That caught the attention of Ford Frick, president of the National League. When Frick heard about the possible boycott, he acted quickly. If any player tried to boycott a game with the Dodgers because of Robinson, Frick said, he would be banned from the game for life. That ended talk of a boycott. Only one game from the series in St. Louis was played due to rain. The Dodgers beat a full Cardinals squad, 4–3, on May 21. Robinson went 0 for 4 with a walk.

Robinson was still hearing abuse from opposing players and fans, and his mail contained all sorts of threats to him and his wife Rachel. He hadn't developed close friendships yet, and when he was in a batting slump, he sat by himself at the far end of the dugout. One writer described Robinson then as "the loneliest man I have ever seen in sports." Interestingly, during one slump Jackie received some tips on hitting from an unexpected source—his teammate, Walker. "Dixie was very difficult at the start, but he was the first guy on the ball club to come to me with advice and help for my hitting," Robinson said. "I knew why—if I helped the ball club, it put money in his pocket. I knew he didn't like me any more in those few short months, but he did come forward."

Along the way, Robinson found time to break another barrier—in the Dodgers' shower room. He had waited until the last white player had used the facilities before showering. One day, outfielder Al Gionfriddo said, "Hey, Robinson. You're as good as anybody else. Come on and take a shower with me."

By the end of May, the worst may have been over for Robinson, and he was ready to display all of his baseball abilities. His batting slump was over, and Jackie was in the lineup to stay. "The guy just had too much talent, and too much guts," Pee Wee Reese said.

As for the team, Brooklyn was in first place by July 1 and stayed there for the rest of the season. Robinson was hitting .314 after that day's game with the Phillies, second on the team to Carl Furillo's .342. The next day turned out to be another landmark event in the history of race relations in major league baseball. On July 2, Robinson had company as an African American in the major leagues.

In an era of personalities, Bill Veeck had one of the biggest. He was a promotional genius who brought Bat Day and Fireworks Night to the game. Veeck took over the Cleveland Indians in 1946, and he was that rare owner who cared only about whether a baseball player could help him win games. Veeck thought he found someone who could do that when he signed Larry Doby to a contract on July 2, 1947. Doby made his debut as a pinch-hitter for the Indians three days later, and Robinson was no longer the only black on a major-league roster. "He's a grand guy and a very good ball player," Robinson said of Doby.

Later in the month, the St. Louis Browns signed African Americans Hank Thompson and Willard Brown. Thompson was only twenty-one years old and a good prospect, while Brown was a veteran. They saw occasional duty for the rest of the season. None of the three players had much of an impact on the pennant race in the American League that

Two pioneers: Jackie Robinson and Larry Doby both broke into the major leagues in 1947.

year, although Doby would soon make his mark. He batted .301 in his first full season with the Indians, helping them win the World Series, the last one captured by Cleveland as of 2015. So Doby was the first black player to win a championship and the first to hit a homer in the Series. He was named an All-Star from 1949 through 1955, and in 1978 he became the second black major-league manager when he was hired by the Chicago White Sox. He was elected to the Baseball Hall of Fame in 1998.

First Black Teammate

In August, Robinson had a new teammate in the person of Dan Bankhead—now remembered as the first black pitcher in major-league history. The Dodgers thought they needed more pitching in the middle of the season, so Bankhead's contract was purchased by the Dodgers from Memphis of the Negro Leagues.

Bankhead didn't have much success with the Dodgers, although he became the first pitcher, white or black, to hit a home run in his first at-bat in big-league history. Negro League star Buck O'Neil thought Bankhead was afraid of hitting a white batter during a game, which Bankhead feared could have led to a riot. "Dan was from Alabama. … He heard all those people calling him names, making those threats, and he was scared. He'd seen black men get lynched," O'Neil said. The first time Bankhead hit an opposing player, there was no reaction—but he didn't pitch well that season.

Bankhead's experience could be considered instructive. There were all sorts of pressures on these men. Some of them weren't quite up to the task at the time. Perhaps the most interesting part of the season isn't that men like Bankhead fell short of success. It's that men like Robinson did overcome those obstacles and did succeed.

The signings did have one obvious meaning, however, no matter how long it took people to grasp it. African-American baseball players were coming, and coming in large numbers. They wouldn't all be instant successes, and they all had to fight off-the-field battles along the way, but it was obvious that blacks were in baseball to stay.

In other words, Jackie Robinson had won his battle. He was quick to share the credit with Rickey. "I think the Rickey Experiment, as I call it, the original idea, would not have come about as successfully with anybody other than Mr. Rickey," he said. "The most important results of it are that it produced understanding among whites, and it gave black people the idea that if I could do it, they could do it, too, that blackness wasn't subservient to anything."

The story, naturally, doesn't end there. Robinson and Doby became good friends, often comparing notes on the obstacles that they faced. They had a lot of similar experiences in 1947 they could share. Robinson was spiked by the Cardinals' Enos Slaughter, which left a 7-inch (18-centimeter) gash in Robinson's leg. Doby once slid into second and had the opposing shortstop spray him with tobacco juice.

Robinson had one experience Doby didn't have: the Dodgers won the National League pennant easily. They extinguished the Cardinals' last hopes by taking two of three games in St. Louis. In the third game, Robinson chased a foul pop to the dugout, jumped in the air to make the catch ... and was caught by Branca before he crashed into the concrete steps. Six months before, Robinson would have wondered if anyone would be there to grab him on such a play.

The team wrapped up the National League title on September 18. The Dodgers were a remarkably balanced unit as all of the regulars contributed. Robinson, however, made a larger impact. His most obvious statistic was his total of stolen bases: twenty-nine. That was more than twice as many as anyone else in the league. Robinson was a threat to steal any time he was on the bases, and he was very difficult to tag when he was in a **rundown**. Robinson was sixth in the league in games played (151 of 154), second in runs (125), ninth in hits (175), and sixth in doubles (31). His .297 batting average was more than satisfactory. The Dodgers set attendance records in every National League ballpark except Crosley Field in Cincinnati. What's more, he had done it under unmatched pressures. The police went through his mail every day to look for death threats. He had garbage, tomatoes, rocks, and watermelon slices thrown at him on the field. Robinson didn't just survive; he starred.

The Dodgers had one more task after the season—a date with the New York Yankees in the World Series. The

Yankees had a superstar in Joe DiMaggio, two other future Hall of Famers on the roster in Phil Rizzuto and a young Yogi Berra, and a star pitcher in Allie Reynolds. Robinson was the center of attention, and he had his mother and mother-in-law fly in from California for the games.

Great to the Finish

An exciting World Series seemed appropriate after all that had happened in 1947, and the Dodgers and Yankees came through. Babe Ruth was in the stands for Game One, the last Series game he attended before dying, and the Yankees won that game and the next one. The Dodgers responded by scoring six runs in the second inning in Game Three and hanging on for a 9–8 win. Game Four featured one of the biggest hits in baseball history. New York's Bill Bevens was one out away from the first no-hitter in World Series history when pinch-hitter Cookie Lavagetto doubled home two runs to give Brooklyn the win. The Yankees took Game Five and seemed poised to rally in Game Six, when Gionfriddo caught a blast by DiMaggio in front of the Yankee bullpen in left field to preserve a Brooklyn victory. It still ranks with the great catches in postseason history. The Dodgers were only a win away from their first World Series victory, but they didn't get it. New York took a 5–2 decision in Game Seven to win the championship.

As for Robinson, he didn't play much of a role in the dramatics of the Series. Jackie did say that he hadn't heard

Jackie Robinson's quickness was on display every time he was caught in a rundown.

so much verbal abuse from an opposing team since the Philadelphia series back in April. He went 7 for 27 (.259) at the plate, scoring three runs and driving in three others. Robinson stole two bases in two tries. The Dodgers are remembered for the fact that they were the first integrated team to take part in the World Series. Only three years later, the last World Series without a black player was staged, as the Yankees beat the Phillies.

When the Series was over, Robinson could finally relax a little. The Baseball Writers' Association of America named him Rookie of the Year in the honor's first year. Robinson also was selected as the second most admirable American in a survey—only entertainer Bing Crosby was ahead of him.

It was quite a year.

Jackie Robinson won the National League's Most Valuable Player award in 1949.

CHAPTER 4
BETTER DAYS

"Every time I look at my pocketbook, I see Jackie Robinson."

—Hall of Fame outfielder Willie Mays

For Jackie Robinson, the best was yet to come.

With 1947 finished, Robinson could look back with pride at becoming a very good player at baseball's highest level. In fact, his play and actions had paved the ways for other African Americans to follow. To use a football phrase—he clearly had moved the ball toward the goal line. This was the time to build on that success.

Robinson showed up for training camp 30 pounds (13.6 kg) overweight in 1948 after a winter of banquets. The man did love to eat. That drew the anger of Dodger manager Leo Durocher, who was back on the job after his one-year suspension. Robinson worked the pounds off in the Florida heat, and the number of race-related incidents had decreased greatly when compared to the 1946 camp in Daytona Beach. That's because team executive Branch Rickey had come up with another idea. It was called "Dodgertown" in Vero Beach.

The complex included baseball diamonds, office facilities, and living quarters for the entire Dodgers organization. Players had little choice but to eat, sleep, and play baseball. While there were benefits to that, the slightly hidden agenda was that the Dodgers' black players were treated just like everyone else in the organization. There were no housing issues or fields that were closed off to them by municipalities. That was an improvement, although Robinson couldn't travel outside the complex easily. Robinson spent spring training playing second base, as Eddie Stanky had been traded and Gil Hodges was placed at first base. Meanwhile, Dixie Walker, who had objected to Robinson's presence in 1947, was traded to Pittsburgh.

The team never quite came together. The biggest development of the year took place on July 16, when the Dodgers had a 36–37 record. Rickey relieved Durocher of his duties and put Burt Shotton back as manager. Durocher was named the new manager of the New York Giants, the Dodgers' biggest rival. Robinson, meanwhile, was slowly winning over his teammates. He quickly became a friend of a midseason addition, pitcher Carl Erskine. "After one game, I walked outside and saw Jack's wife, Rachel, and son Jackie Jr. waiting for him," Erskine told *Sports Illustrated* later. "So I went over to say hello. Later, Jack thanked me and told me how much it meant to him that I spoke to his family in front of his friends. To me, it was as natural as taking a breath."

Robinson turned in another solid season in 1948. He hit .296 with twelve homers and a team-leading eighty-five runs batted in (RBIs). As the 1949 season approached, Robinson had turned thirty and knew more about the game and the league. He spent hours working with legendary hitter George Sisler before the season. When the season began, Robinson and the Dodgers were ready to begin a run of dramatic years.

Given a Voice

The 1949 season was the best of Robinson's career—perhaps, in part, because Rickey gave Robinson permission to fight back. Rickey said, "You're earned the right to be yourself, Jackie. You've given so much to the game that you are now in a position to comport yourself as other players do."

Robinson's voice was heard on the field and from the dugout. Robinson raised his batting average to a league-leading .342, stole a league-leading thirty-seven bases, scored a career-best 122 runs, and drove in a career-best 124 runs. Robinson was one of four black players to be selected to the National League team for the 1949 All-Star Game; teammates Roy Campanella and Don Newcombe also were picked. After the season, Robinson was selected as the National League's Most Valuable Player.

Robinson had one large distraction during the course of the season. He was called to testify before the **House Un-American Activities Committee** in Washington, DC. Robinson thought about declining but believed such a move might hurt his career. He was asked about comments coming from black actor and athlete Paul Robeson, who said black Americans would never fight an imperialist war for their country. Robinson responded by saying he would fight racism and segregation in order to create change in the United States.

The Dodgers as a team never had more than a two-and-a-half-game lead in the final weeks of the season, but they held off the St. Louis Cardinals to win the pennant by a game. Brooklyn couldn't beat the Yankees in the World Series again, losing in five games.

The beat went on for Robinson when the calendar flipped to the 1950s. Jackie hit .328 in 1950 and was part of a stunning late-season comeback that fell just short. Brooklyn trailed Philadelphia by seven games with twelve to play, yet cut the lead to two games with two games left to play against the Phillies at home. The Dodgers won the first game, but Philadelphia took the season's final game and the pennant on a three-run homer in the tenth inning by George Sisler's son, Dick.

At year's end, part-owner Walter O'Malley bought out Rickey's financial interest to gain full control of the team. The two men did not get along, and O'Malley sent Rickey out the door. That ended an era in the franchise's history. Robinson was always quick to acknowledge Rickey's huge role in integrating major league baseball. Rickey had the courage and the imagination needed to reach that important goal.

Giants Win the Pennant

Robinson turned in another superb season in 1951, and his team was involved in one of the great pennant races in history. Brooklyn looked like an easy winner when it was thirteen and a half games ahead of the Giants. But New York won sixteen straight games and spent the rest of the season closing in. On the last day of the season, the Dodgers needed to win in Philadelphia to force a best-of-three playoff for the title. Robinson made a game-saving catch in the bottom of the twelfth inning. Then he hit the most dramatic home run of his life in the fourteenth inning to give Brooklyn the win. It was the most exciting game anyone could remember … for less than a week.

The Giants and Dodgers split the first two games in the playoff, and it looked like Brooklyn was headed to the World Series when it led in the bottom of the ninth. But Bobby Thomson—who had played for Jersey City in Robinson's first game for Montreal—of the Giants hit a three-run homer to win it in one of the most famous moments in baseball history. As Thomson ran around the bases, Robinson stood at second base amidst the bedlam, checking to make sure Thomson touched all of the bags.

By 1952, Robinson still was cranking out good seasons as if they came out of a copy machine. He always hit above .300, always drove in a bunch of runs, always was on the All-Star team, and always was a contender for Most Valuable Player honors. However, the results in the fall were depressingly similar as well—the Dodgers kept falling just short of their first World Series title. In 1952, the Yankees won the Series in seven games.

Robinson created some controversy that year when he called Yankees general manager George Weiss a bigot. The Yankees were still three years away from having a black player on their roster. While the tone might have been unusual, the outburst couldn't have surprised his fellow Dodgers. Usually Robinson was more than willing to speak his mind, particularly in the clubhouse. He'd often raise his voice and become angry, which drew this response from teammate Newcombe: "Robinson, not only are you wrong, you're loud wrong." Jackie never tired of raising his voice against what he perceived to be injustice in society.

The Dodgers continued their run of excellent seasons in 1953, losing to the Yankees again in the World Series. Robinson started to serve as more of a utility man that year, moving around to different positions. Brooklyn wasn't good enough to stop the Giants—still managed by Durocher—from winning in 1954.

Moment of Triumph

By 1955, the heart of the team was nearing the end of a spectacular decade, and time was running out on this special group. Robinson was thirty-six, and his gray hair led his teammates to good-naturedly call him "**Uncle Remus**." That made the 1955 season all the more surprising. The Dodgers got off to one of the great starts in baseball history. Brooklyn was 22–2 on May 10, and the pennant race was virtually over. Brooklyn wrapped up the title on September 8. For his part, Robinson finally showed signs of decline, hitting .256 in 317 at-bats.

The Yankees again were waiting in the World Series. Robinson provided the most famous moment of his postseason career in Game One. After hitting a triple, he took off from third base in the eighth inning in an attempt to steal home. Yankee catcher Yogi Berra caught the pitch from Whitey Ford, Robinson slid into the base, umpire Bill Summers called Robinson safe … and Berra went wild. You've never seen an angrier man than Berra. Even so, the Dodgers lost that game to the Yankees and lost the next one, too. The Dodgers rallied to set up a Game Seven in Yankee Stadium. But the Yankees always won Game Seven, didn't they? Not this time. Johnny Podres pitched a complete game for a 2–0 win, and the Dodgers were World Champions for the first time in their history. Robinson didn't play in Game Seven, but he had a new title: World Champion.

The Dodgers came back in 1956 to defend their World Series title and held off Milwaukee and Cincinnati to take another pennant. Robinson hit .275 in 117 games and still had enough speed at thirty-seven to steal twelve bases. The Yankees were waiting in the Series again. The teams split the first six games of the competition, with Don Larsen's perfect game for New York providing an all-time highlight in Game Five. (No one else has pitched a complete game in a World Series without allowing a base runner.) Back in Brooklyn, Robinson perhaps had the best World Series moment of his career. His walk-off hit in Game Six, a liner over the head of Enos Slaughter in the bottom of the tenth inning gave the Dodgers a 1–0 victory. But Brooklyn had nothing left the next day and dropped a 9–0 decision to lose the Series.

Jackie Robinson steals home against the New York Yankees in the 1955 World Series, despite the efforts of Yankees catcher Yogi Berra.

8
Dodgers

Robinson knew his playing days were about over, and he decided he didn't have any interest in managing. Yet his departure from baseball was stunning, and the events surrounding it were controversial. Robinson had signed a contract to announce the retirement exclusively in *Look* magazine, as he was taking a job as an executive with the Chock full o'Nuts Company. The firm had a chain of coffee shops in the New York City area. The contract was signed in early December, about a month before the story was to appear in *Look*. The ink on the deal with *Look* was barely dry that day when Robinson received a message to call the Dodgers. He found out he had been traded to, of all teams, their archrivals, the New York Giants. Robinson, who hadn't gotten along with O'Malley, was looking for some security in his life and didn't think baseball could provide it. Robinson couldn't tell the Giants he was leaving baseball because of his contract with the magazine. After the *Look* story was published, Dodgers general manager Buzzie Bavasi charged that Robinson was using the retirement threat to get a better contract. Robinson told a reporter he might have been talked into playing for the Giants, but after Bavasi's stinging words, he vowed to never play again. He filed his retirement papers several days later, fulfilling his vow.

A Public Figure

As Robinson entered the next phase of his life, diabetes was a big part of the picture for him. He received insulin treatments for the disease, but researchers had not made great advances at that point. Therefore, his body would slowly fail him. Even so, Robinson threw himself into a variety of projects. For the rest of his life, he remained competitive, outspoken, and combative.

He stayed with Chock full o'Nuts until 1964, and he was called the first black person to become a vice president of a major American corporation. Robinson said he thought it was his job to help black people make progress in business, and he worked on personnel matters.

In addition, he became active in politics for the rest of his life. Robinson surprised many people when he backed Richard M. Nixon for president in the 1960 election. John F. Kennedy had told Robinson that he didn't know much about the problems of blacks, and that offended Robinson. However, Kennedy won that election, and Robinson later expressed support for Kennedy's actions on civil rights. Robinson constantly wrote letters to people and groups to advance his viewpoints on the subject.

In 1964, Robinson became one of the founders of the Freedom National Bank— a black-owned and -operated bank that was based in Harlem. He worked on behalf of New York Governor Nelson Rockefeller's campaign for the Presidency that year, and he later landed a position with Rockefeller as New York state's special assistant for community affairs. Robinson also made other investments in a variety of businesses.

Robinson's connections to baseball were rare after his retirement from the game. He served as a television

Baseball commissioner Bowie Kuhn (*right*) honored Jackie Robinson before the second game of the 1972 World Series. Robinson threw out the ceremonial first pitch.

commentator twice, once for ABC. He appeared at the 1972 World Series, throwing out the first pitch before Game Two. Robinson accepted a plaque to celebrate the twenty-fifth anniversary of his arrival in the major leagues. He took the opportunity to point out that there had never been a black manager in the major leagues: "I'm going to be tremendously more pleased and more proud when I look at that third base coaching line one day and see a black face managing in baseball."

By that time, Robinson's time was almost up. His health had been deteriorating for some time, and now his eyesight was almost gone. Nine days after the World Series appearance, he suffered a heart attack. Robinson died on October 24, 1972.

GAME-CHANGING CHRONOLOGY

January 31, 1919: Born in Cairo, Georgia.

1920: Moves to Pasadena, California.

1937: Graduates from John Muir Technical High School.

1937–1939: Attends Pasadena Junior College.

1939–1941: Attends UCLA.

April 3, 1942: Inducted into the United States Army.

August 2, 1944: Cleared of all charges after a court-martial.

November 28, 1944: Discharged from the army.

1945: Signs with the Kansas City Monarchs of the Negro Leagues.

August 28, 1945: Agrees to join Brooklyn Dodgers after meeting with Branch Rickey.

October 23, 1945: Dodgers announce signing of Robinson.

February 10, 1946: Marries Rachel Isum.

April 18, 1946: Debuts for Montreal in a game at Jersey City.

April 15, 1947: Debuts for Brooklyn in a game against Boston.

July 2, 1947: Larry Doby signs with the Cleveland Indians.

July 12, 1949: Plays in first All-Star Game.

October 4, 1955: Robinson and Dodgers win World Series.

January 5, 1957: Formally retires from baseball.

October 15, 1972: Makes final public appearance at World Series.

October 24, 1972: Dies in North Stamford, Connecticut.

Jackie Robinson paved the way for African-American stars such as Hank Aaron and Willie Mays to play major-league baseball.

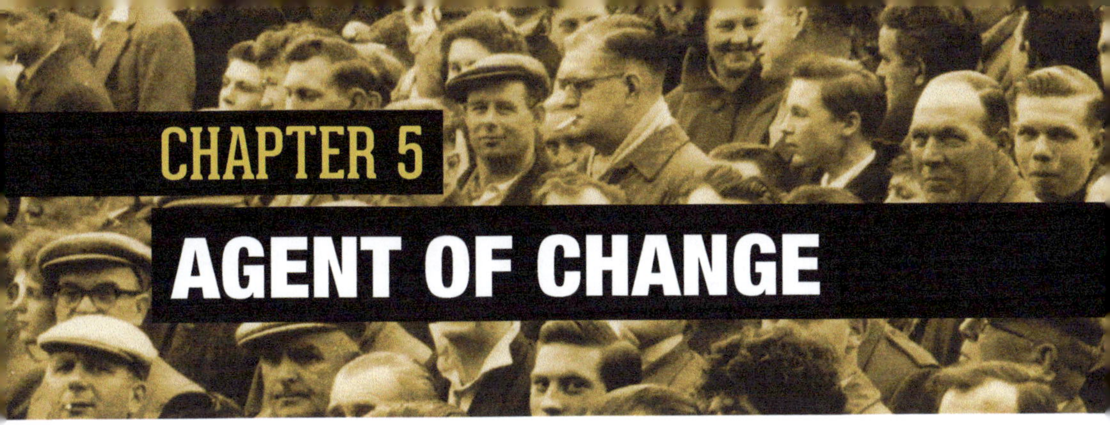

CHAPTER 5

AGENT OF CHANGE

"The word for Jackie Robinson is 'unconquerable.' ... He would not be defeated."

–sportswriter Red Smith

When it comes to Jackie Robinson's legacy, the starting point of any discussion is quite simple.

He is the most important cultural figure in the history of American sports. When Robinson entered major league baseball in 1947, American race relations had been at a virtual standstill since the Civil War. By the time Robinson left baseball, the United States was moving toward equality. Jackie wasn't the only reason for that, but the role he played was huge.

Let's start with the fact that baseball really was America's national pastime then. The game dominated the landscape, as pro football was just starting to catch on, pro basketball was barely organized, and hockey was popular only in a few cold-weather cities. When World War II ended, America could afford to pay attention to leisure sports again—the war had followed the Great Depression, so millions of families couldn't afford to play or watch baseball for years. However, the major leagues were for whites only, with blacks having their own leagues. There were exhibition games in the 1930s between white and black teams, and both sides knew about the great players on the other side, but there was also plenty of hatred in society that poisoned everything it touched, and it touched many aspects of life.

Along came Robinson in 1947. Unlike a handful of blacks who claimed they were Native American or Cuban in an attempt to play baseball in the nineteenth century, Robinson did not hide his race. There he was, on the field with an otherwise all-white team. Then when he left the field, he traveled with them as a group on road trips, stayed with them (when he could) in hotels, and ate with them (when he could) in restaurants.

Four great baseball players—Frank Robinson, Hank Aaron, Willie Mays, and Barry Bonds—share a laugh at a 2002 event honoring Bonds. Robinson became baseball's first black manager with Cleveland in 1975.

Slowly but surely, people realized that this was no big deal. The idea probably started with his teammates, and it took them a while to figure it out. But in most cases they did. Dixie Walker, his teammate from 1947 who started a petition to keep him off the team, later told sportswriter Roger Kahn, "It was the dumbest thing I ever did in my life. Would you tell everybody that I'm deeply sorry?"

Bobby Bragan, another member of that Dodger team who wasn't happy about playing with Robinson, said Jackie won him over in no time. "It took about four weeks, I'd say, for Jackie to convince all of us—Yankees, Southerners, or whatever—and we were fighting each other then, to get to sit with him in the dining car," he said. "He made me a better man, and I was really grateful to him."

Successful Experiment

Robinson changed minds and attitudes every day. Fifteen of the baseball owners—every one but Brooklyn's—had voted in 1946 not to integrate the sport before Robinson's arrival. Yet by the middle of the 1947 season, some of those same owners had signed other black players to contracts. "The Great Experiment" was working.

"When you're a part of history, you're too close to it and you don't see it," teammate Carl Erskine told *Sports Illustrated*. "I was aware of the flow—Robinson, Campanella, Newcombe—these guys were great ballplayers. Sports at the major league level provides one of the purest settings there is. You have to produce. Nobody can help you. Favoritism

Jackie Robinson was an activist outside of the baseball diamond for much of his life.

does you no good. Baseball integration sped up the whole integration process because it provided direct proof that blacks were qualified."

Soon, other "experiments" were taking place. One of the biggest took place in 1948, when President Harry Truman completely integrated the armed forces. Would that have happened without Robinson? Certainly blacks were angry after World War II, when they returned to an America where many couldn't vote, get a good education, or eat at a public restaurant. Robinson had shown that integration was possible in one area of life, and Truman took another step down the road to equality.

It wasn't long before the concept of "separate but equal"—the law of the land for the first half of the twentieth century when it came to race relations—was challenged in the courts. While educational systems for blacks and whites were often separate, they were far from equal. This arrangement was declared illegal in a 1954 decision of the Supreme Court. Only a year before Robinson's 1956 retirement, Rosa Parks was arrested for not moving to the back of a Montgomery, Alabama, bus. It was the same so-called offense that got Robinson into trouble in the army.

Bus segregation was declared unconstitutional just before Robinson's retirement. From there, other civil rights laws followed. It was far from easy, as the battle for equality featured some of the ugliest moments in our nation's history—but change did arrive.

Today we're still fighting some of those battles for equal rights. However, America is a much better place in terms of race than it was in 1947, and Robinson deserves some of the credit. In fact, it could be argued that a line could be drawn from Jackie Robinson to Dr. Martin Luther King Jr. to President Barack Obama.

Next, let's look at what happened to a couple of crucial parts of Robinson's life: the Negro Leagues and the Brooklyn Dodgers. Both were gone shortly after Robinson retired.

End of Negro Leagues

As soon as Robinson signed with the Dodgers, owners of teams in the Negro Leagues should have known they were doomed. Attendance immediately dropped. The Negro Leagues had many years of tradition on their side, but when the major leagues integrated, young blacks had to make a decision about where they would play. That ultimately came down to dollars, and the majors had a lot more of them. Not only would the stars slowly peel away from the Negro League rosters, but the prospects coming out of high school would sign with major-league teams as well. The Negro League owners were in a tough spot. If they kept their best players, they were preventing progress for an entire race. If they let them go, they suffered severe financial losses. When top players did leave, the Negro League teams often didn't receive any money from the major-league teams. The Negro American League was the only group of its kind by 1949, and the quality of play kept dropping until it folded in 1958.

As for the Dodgers, cultural changes were at work in their demise. Home attendance in 1947, boosted by Robinson's arrival and a pennant-winning team, was 1.8 million. For the rest of Robinson's career, the team was almost always very good, usually in a pennant race, sometimes the National League champion, and once a World Series winner. It should have been extremely difficult to find an unsold seat in Ebbets Field for a decade.

But it wasn't. Attendance had a brief spurt to 1.6 million in 1949, but it never reached that height again. The numbers for Brooklyn were between 1 million and 1.3 million through 1956. Meanwhile, the Milwaukee Braves had found new life after moving from Boston, where they drew 281,000 in their final season there in 1952. The Braves attracted 1.8 million fans in 1953 and went past the 2 million mark from 1954 to 1956.

Brooklyn owner Walter O'Malley couldn't keep up with Milwaukee's economic muscle, and he didn't like his team's long-term financial outlook. The Dodgers moved into Ebbets Field in 1913. It was in a classic city location of its time, which meant it was built without any parking lots. Fans used public transportation to attend games for decades, but that was changing quickly in the 1950s. People were leaving New York City to live in the suburbs, and once there they needed cars to get around. It was difficult for fans to drive to a Dodgers' game in this era as highways became crowded, and there was no place to park when they got there. Some fans preferred to just stay home and watch the Dodgers on television—a device that would change the culture in then-unimagined ways. Meanwhile, city neighborhoods started to decline economically because people who moved were often better off financially than the ones who stayed.

O'Malley tried to get a new stadium, one with plenty of parking, and got nowhere. The city fathers of New York were in no hurry to help. O'Malley was offered land in Flushing Meadows, where the New York Mets play now, but he wanted property in Brooklyn. Talks eventually broke down. At the same time, the New York Giants had the same problems. They had an ancient stadium, the Polo Grounds, located in what was fast becoming a slum. New York drew a million fans in a season only once between 1951 and 1957.

Lure of the West

The solution for O'Malley came from the West. Los Angeles was a growing city and wanted a big-league baseball team. Commercial air travel had become efficient enough for teams to make the trip to the West Coast easily. Talk of moving the team may have started out as a bluff, but negotiations between O'Malley and Los Angeles eventually turned serious. A catch was that having one team more than 1,000 miles (1,609 km) from any other franchise made little sense, so the Giants agreed to move to San Francisco. Right after the end of the 1957 season, New York lost both of its National League baseball teams. The twin moves really were the signal of major changes to Major League Baseball, including the addition of eight new teams in the 1960s.

Interestingly enough, the Braves—whose popularity in their new city started all of this—were over two million in attendance in 1957 when they won the World Series. However, they fell below that number in 1958 despite winning another pennant. By 1962, Milwaukee only attracted 766,000. The Braves moved to Atlanta in 1966. Other teams moved as well during that era—the St. Louis Browns headed for Baltimore in 1954, the Philadelphia Athletics went to Kansas City in 1955, and Washington, DC, transferred to Minnesota in 1961.

No matter where those teams played, they had an increasing number of black athletes on their rosters. Robinson's biggest effect on baseball came with the players who followed him. Obviously, the major league teams—well, some of them at least—went after the best players and best prospects from the pool of African-American players first. The list started with Larry Doby, who later was inducted into the Hall of Fame.

What would we have missed if black players hadn't been around? Look at the list of most valuable players in the National League, starting with Robinson in 1949.

Black players include Roy Campanella (1951, 1953, and 1955), Willie Mays (1954), Hank Aaron (1957), Ernie Banks (1958 and 1959), and Frank Robinson (1961). Four of the last five teams to put a black player in their uniforms were from the American League—the Senators, Yankees, Tigers, and Red Sox.

Jackie Robinson was the first of them elected to the Hall of Fame. He went in the first year he was eligible (players must be retired for five years before they are eligible for induction). Since then, all of those former MVPs and dozens of other black players have been enshrined. Among them were some of the Negro League players who were denied a chance to play in the majors.

Change of Speeds

Robinson also brought a different style of play along with him when he arrived from the Negro Leagues. To explain that, we need a quick lesson in how the game was played.

Before 1920, baseball often was played to score one run at a time. Teams scratched out a hit, and then did what it took to score—like stealing a base or sacrificing. It was called "scientific baseball," and it was hard work. But then Babe Ruth turned up as a full-time hitter, and fans turned out in large numbers to see the "Sultan of Swat" hammer the ball into the seats. Ruth hit fifty-four homers for the Yankees in 1920, with George Sisler second with nineteen. Baseball management got rid of the spitball, put a little more bounce into the baseball, and watched the runs score.

Still, the Negro Leagues never took that change in the game completely to heart. Yes, there were some sluggers there, but their game emphasized speed. Robinson played only a season in the Negro Leagues, but he fit right in. As a Dodger, he was always a threat to steal a base or go from first to third on a teammate's hit. It was a different way of playing. African American Sam Jethroe was thirty-three when he reached the big leagues with the Boston Braves in 1950, and he was named NL rookie of the year after stealing thirty-five bases. He matched that total the next year, leading the league both seasons. The stolen base totals for the sport kept going up and up through the 1940s and the 1950s. In 1962, African American Maury Wills stole 104 bases to break Ty Cobb's record for steals in a season (ninety-six in 1915).

People had noticed the lack of black managers in major league baseball, but no one did anything about it before Robinson called for change in 1972. Jackie's words increased the pressure on owners, but he didn't live to see such a hiring take place. Frank Robinson, one of Jackie's successors on the field, became the first black manager in major-league history when he was hired to lead the Cleveland Indians in 1975.

Jackie Robinson's contributions to the game and to the country were almost instantly recognized. He went into the Baseball Hall of Fame as soon as he was eligible in 1962, the first African American to be so honored. At the time, there were still state universities in this country in which blacks weren't welcome. He received all sorts of

Maury Wills followed in Jackie Robinson's footsteps and became one of baseball's greatest base stealers.

honors over the years, including the Congressional Medal of Honor and the Presidential Medal of Freedom.

Number 42

The Dodgers retired his uniform number in 1972, but a greater honor was ahead. Uniform number 42 was retired throughout major league baseball in 1997, the fiftieth anniversary of Robinson's debut. It's the only baseball-wide action of its kind. Players who had been wearing number 42 were allowed to keep it, and thus New York Yankees pitcher Mariano Rivera—himself a great player—became the last man to wear it when he retired in 2013.

Speaking of uniforms, UCLA decided to honor Robinson in a unique way. The school's athletic teams all retired number 42 in 2014, even though he didn't wear the number there. UCLA officials said number 42 was closely associated with Robinson. The announcement came on the seventy-fifth anniversary of Robinson's arrival at the Westwood campus.

Robinson is one of a handful of players to be named both Rookie of the Year and Most Valuable Player. Since he was the first Rookie of the Year in 1947, it's only fitting that the award is now named after him. If you like your heroes on a postage stamp, Robinson is a good choice. He's been on three of them. How about in the movies? Robinson's story has been told by Hollywood a few times, including 2013's *42*, featuring Chadwick Boseman as

OTHER PIONEERS

We know Jackie Robinson broke the color line in major league baseball. What about the other major team sports? They should be remembered, too.

Football

Charles Follis is believed to have been the first black professional football player, playing for the Shelby Steamfitters from 1902 to 1906. A handful of blacks played in the predecessor of the National Football League in the 1920s, but they were all out of the game by 1927. A few others popped up during the next few years. However, none played from 1933 to 1945.

Kenny Washington signed with the Los Angeles Rams in 1946, and Woody Strode followed shortly after that. The first black to be picked in the NFL draft was George Taliaferro, who went in the thirteenth round in 1949 to the Chicago Bears.

Basketball

Three players share the distinction of integrating the National Basketball Association in 1950. Chuck Cooper might have the biggest honor, since he was the first black to be drafted when the Boston Celtics picked him in the second round. However, Nat "Sweetwater" Clifton was the first African American to sign with an NBA team (New York Knickerbockers), and Earl Lloyd was the first black to play in an actual game (Washington Capitols).

Hockey

Willie O'Ree broke the color line in the National Hockey League on January 18, 1958, when he played for the Boston Bruins. The first US-born black athlete to play in the NHL (O'Ree was born in Canada) was Val James, who suited up for the Buffalo Sabres in 1982. Mike Grier is considered the first black hockey player born and trained in the United States to reach the NHL, joining the Edmonton Oilers in 1996.

EDD J. ROUSH
CHICAGO A.L. 1913
JACK ROOSEVELT ROBINSON
BROOKLYN N.L. 1947 TO 1956
LEADING N.L. BATTER IN 1949. HOLDS
FIELDING MARK FOR SECOND BASEMAN
PLAYING IN 150 OR MORE GAMES WITH .992.
LEAD N.L. IN STOLEN BASES IN 1947 AND
1949. MOST VALUABLE PLAYER IN 1949.
LIFETIME BATTING AVERAGE .311. JOINT
RECORD HOLDER FOR MOST DOUBLE PLAYS
BY SECOND BASEMAN, 137 IN 1951.
LED SECOND BASEMEN IN DOUBLE
PLAYS 1949-50-51-52.

Edd Roush, Jackie Robinson, Bob Feller, and Bill McKechnie entered the Hall of Fame together in 1962.

Jackie and Harrison Ford as Branch Rickey. A Broadway musical about his life was produced in 1987.

Then there are the statues. Robinson is honored in that way in Pasadena, with 9-footers (2.7 m) of Jackie and brother Mack right across the street from City Hall. Daytona Beach put up a statue of Robinson and a young boy outside its baseball stadium. When the Los Angeles Dodgers decided to begin a tradition of honoring their greatest players in 2015 with a statue at Dodger Stadium, Robinson was the first choice.

Jackie and Rachel had three children: Sharon, David, and Jackie Jr. Sharon has held a variety of positions, including director of educational programming for Major League Baseball. She has written two books about her father. David has been described as a social activist in Tanzania; he also grows coffee. However, Jackie Robinson Jr.'s story didn't come out so happily. He had emotional problems while growing up, was wounded while serving in the armed forces in Vietnam in 1965, and developed substance abuse problems. His father spent many of his later years fighting against drug abuse. At the age of twenty-four, Jackie Jr. was killed in a car accident after falling asleep while driving.

"You don't know what it's like to lose a son, find him, and lose him again," Jackie Sr. said. "My problem was my inability to spend much time at home. I thought my family was secure, so I went running around every place else. I guess I had more of an effect on other people's kids than I did my own."

Jackie couldn't have picked a better person than wife Rachel to represent him after his passing. She founded the Jackie Robinson Foundation and continued to represent his ideals beautifully well into her nineties. The foundation awards college scholarships to underserved populations. In 2013–2014 alone, it provided $4 million in scholarship assistance and program support.

As for Jackie himself, he was buried in Cypress Hills Cemetery in Brooklyn. He's next to his son and mother-in-law. Twenty-five years later, the Interboro Parkway—which splits the cemetery in two—was renamed the Jackie Robinson Parkway.

GLOSSARY

balk An illegal action by a baseball pitcher that is considered a deliberate attempt to deceive the other team. All base runners move up one base as a penalty when a balk is called by umpires.

Battle of the Bulge The last major German offensive of World War II (December 1944 to January 1945) inflicted heavy casualties on United States forces.

cane syrup A thick liquid created when juice is boiled out of sugarcane over the course of several hours.

color line Refers to the separation of blacks and whites in American society after the end of the Civil War.

court-martial A military court that reviews possible violations of military law and punishes those found guilty.

cross A symbol of Christianity. The Ku Klux Klan, a hate group that had a large following between World War I and World War II, sometimes burned crosses in front of the houses of its "enemies" in an attempt to intimidate them.

Custer's Last Stand Also known as the Battle of Little Bighorn, this military battle featured a one-sided victory by three Native American tribes over the Seventh Cavalry led by US General George Custer in 1876. It took place in Eastern Montana.

discrimination A way of placing people or groups at a competitive disadvantage without regard to their individual merit or merits. In the baseball sense, black athletes were not given the opportunity to play in the major leagues for decades only because of their skin color and in spite of their abilities.

GI Bill A 1944 law designed to help returning veterans from World War II. Benefits included low-cost mortgages, payments for collegiate or vocational training, and a year of unemployment compensation.

House Un-American Activities Committee A committee from the House of Representatives mostly associated with investigating disloyalty by private citizens during the 1940s and 1950s.

pennant The championship of a league but not an overall title. Baseball's American League and National League champions each win a pennant before they meet in the World Series.

rundown A situation in baseball when a runner is caught between bases and in danger of being tagged out.

segregated Restricted to one group. The word is often used about races of people, when they are kept apart from each other either in housing or in public facilities.

GLOSSARY

Uncle Remus A fictional character from African-American folk stories, adapted and popularized by Joel Chandler Harris starting in the 1880s. He is usually portrayed as a gray-haired, older gentleman who is considered kind and wise by all who know him.

welfare Provides citizens with a minimum level of financial and social support, particularly those with children.

SELECTED BIBLIOGRAPHY

BOOKS

Eig, Jonathan. *Opening Day: The Story of Jackie Robinson's First Season*. New York: Simon & Schuster, 2007.

James, Bill. *The New Bill James Historical Baseball Abstract.* New York: Free Press, 2001.

Kahn, Roger. *The Era, 1947–1957: When the Yankees, the Giants, and the Dodgers Ruled the World.* New York: Ticknor & Fields, 1993.

———. *Rickey & Robinson: The True, Untold Story of the Integration of Baseball.* New York: Rodale, 2014.

Koppett, Leonard. *Koppett's Concise History of Major League Baseball.* Philadelphia, PA: Temple University Press, 1998.

Rampersad, Arnold. *Jackie Robinson: A Biography*. New York: Knopf, 1997.

Robinson, Jackie. *Baseball Has Done It*. New York: Ig Publishing, 2005.

Robinson, Jackie, as told to Alfred Duckett. *I Never Had It Made*. Hopewell, NJ: Ecco Press, 1995.

Simon, Scott. *Jackie Robinson and the Integration of Baseball.* Hoboken, NJ: Wiley & Sons, 2002.

Tygiel, Jules, ed. *The Jackie Robinson Reader: Perspectives on an American Hero*. New York: Penguin Books, 1997.

Ward, Geoffrey C., and Ken Burns. *Baseball: An Illustrated History*. New York: Knopf, 1994.

SELECTED BIBLIOGRAPHY

ONLINE ARTICLES

Anderson, Dave. "Jackie Robinson, First Black in Major League, Dies." *New York Times*, October 25, 1972. Accessed May 10, 2015. www.nytimes.com/learning/general/onthisday/bday/0131.html

Cronin, Brian. "Did Reese really embrace Robinson in '47?" ESPN.com, April 13, 2010. Accessed May 2, 2015. espn.go.com/blog/playbook/fandom/post/_/id/20917/did-reese-really-embrace-robinson-in-47

Herzog, Brad. "A Home Run for the Ages." *Sports Illustrated*, April 1, 1996. Accessed May 7, 2015. www.si.com/vault/1996/04/01/211556/a-home-run-for-the-ages-jackie-robinsons-first-minor-league-game-50-years-ago-was-a-major-event

Nack, William. "The Breakthrough." *Sports Illustrated*, May 5, 1997. Accessed May 2, 2015. www.si.com/mlb/2015/04/15/jackie-robinson-day-william-nack-si-vault

Rollins, Jimmy. "A Special Day to be a Dodger." *Sports Illustrated*, April 15, 2015. Accessed May 2, 2015. www.si.com/mlb/2015/04/15/jimmy-rollins-jackie-robinson-dodgers

Stilley, Aaron. "Jackie Robinson & The 1945 Kansas City Monarchs." *I-70 Baseball*, Dec. 1, 2010. Accessed May 2, 2015.www.i70baseball.com/2010/12/01/jackie-robinson-the-1945-kansas-city-monarchs/

FURTHER INFORMATION

Books

Kahn, Roger. *The Boys of Summer*. Reissue edition. New York: Harper Perennial Modern Classics, 2008.

Tygiel, Jules. *Baseball's Great Experiment: Jackie Robinson and His Legacy.* Oxford, England. Oxford University Press, 2008.

Ward, Geoffrey C., Ken Burns, and Kevin Baker. *Baseball: An Illustrated History.* Reprint edition. New York: Knopf, 2010.

Video

Jackie Robinson Steals Home
www.youtube.com/watch?v=6XY-XshGhMU
Watch black-and-white footage of Jackie Robinson stealing home in the 1955 World Series against the New York Yankees.

Jackie Robinson SportsCentury
www.youtube.com/watch?v=DfoVWerv2S8
ESPN's SportsCentury series includes an eleven-minute segment on the man who broke baseball's color barrier.

The Jackie Robinson Story
www.youtube.com/watch?v=gNm-UlJmKUg
Watch the entire 1950 movie made about the life of young Jackie Robinson, courtesy of YouTube.

FURTHER INFORMATION

SEA@LAD Dodgers Celebrate Jackie Robinson Day

www.youtube.com/watch?v=qD_qy-SpSYQ

This video shows a Major League Baseball celebration of Jackie Robinson Day, featuring team owner Magic Johnson, former pitcher Sandy Koufax, first black manager Frank Robinson, and Rachel Robinson.

USC vs UCLA 1939 – Jackie Robinson #28

www.youtube.com/watch?v=gMyngKxvJ4s

Explore a video of a 0–0 tie played between the University of Southern California and the University of California Los Angeles football teams. It shows that Jackie Robinson was more than just a baseball player.

Organizations

Baseball Reference

www.baseball-reference.com

The Jackie Robinson Foundation

www.jackierobinson.org.

National Baseball Hall of Fame

www.baseballhall.org

Negro Leagues Baseball Museum

www.nlbm.com

Society for American Baseball Research

www.sabr.org

INDEX

Page numbers in **boldface** are illustrations. Entries in **boldface** are glossary terms.

INDEX

ABOUT THE AUTHOR

Budd Bailey has been a sports reporter and editor at the *Buffalo News* since 1993. Before that, Budd worked for the Buffalo Sabres hockey team and for WEBR Radio, where he served as one of the announcers for the Buffalo Bisons' baseball team for four seasons. Budd and his wife, Jody, live in Buffalo, New York.